D0805516

# MANX ARE THE BEST!

Elaine Landau

LERNER PUBLICATIONS COMPANY · MINNEAPOLIS

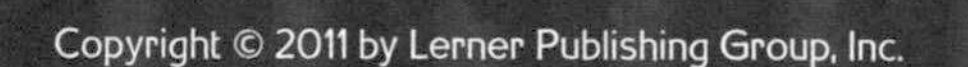



Lerner Publications Company
A division of Lerner Publishing Group, Inc.
241 First Avenue North
Minneapolis, MN 55401 U.S.A.

Website address: www.lernerbooks.com

Library of Congress Cataloging-in-Publication Data

Landau, Elaine.
Manx are the best! / by Elaine Landau.
p. cm. — (The best cats ever)
Includes index.
ISBN 978-0-7613-6432-0 (lib. bdg. : alk. paper)
1. Manx cat—Juvenile literature. I. Title.
SF449.M36L36 2011
636.8'22-dc22 2010024224

Manufactured in the United States of America
1 - CG - 12/31/10

# TABLE OF CONTENTS

CHAPTER ONE

# A VERY PRETTY KITTY

What a good-looking cat! Check out its nicely curved body, thick fur, and large eyes. From the front, there's nothing too unusual about this kitty—other than how very pretty it is. But wait! It's turning around. Surprise! That cat has no tail. It must be a **Manx**.

## Not Your Average Cat

A Manx has a special look. You don't see many tailless kitties. The Manx's body is different in another way too. Its hind legs are longer than its front legs. These cats tend to hop as they walk. Some people say they move like bunny rabbits.

## Are Manx Cats Always Tailless?

Nope. In one Manx litter, you can have all these different types of cats:

**rumpy:** a completely tailless Manx

**riser:** a Manx with just the start of a tail under its skin. You may feel this tail, but you can't see it.

**stumpy:** a Manx with a very short tail

**longy:** a Manx with a longer tail

All these types of Manx make great pets—but only a rumpy or a riser can be entered in cat shows.

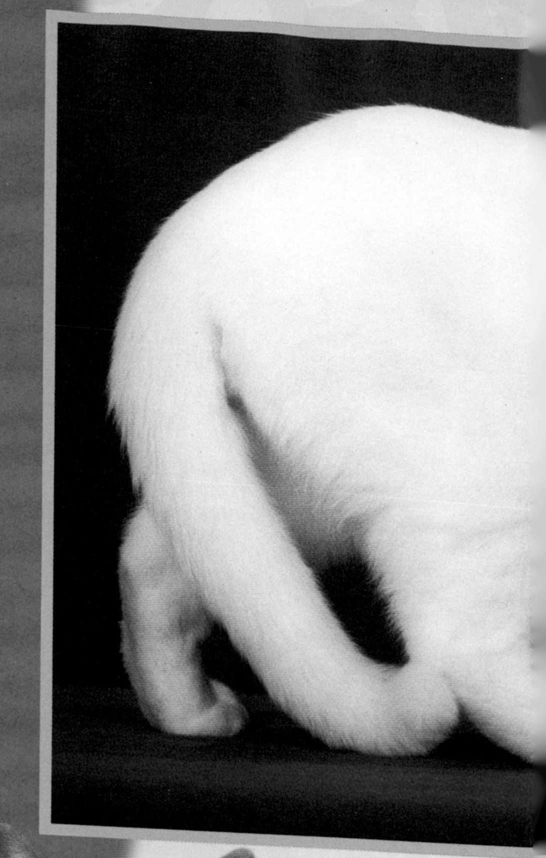

This Manx is a stumpy. The Manx above is a longy.

Manx cats come in a variety of colors. They may be a solid color or mixed colors. They may be shorthaired or longhaired. But all these furry felines have one thing in common. They are lovely to look at.

## A Cat with Charm

Yet the Manx has more than a pretty face and an interesting body. These cats are also smart, active, and playful. Manx cats have been described as charming.

## The Best Name

Give your super cat the best name ever. Do any of these fit your Manx?

Peaches
Sabrina
Dolly
Barney
Orion
Louie
Joey
Bella
Princess
Dumpling

Some people say Manx cats act more like dogs than cats. They come when called, and they often follow their owners around the house. Their owners think they have the best cats ever. It's easy to see why!

A Manx goes to its owner when it is called, just like a dog!

CHAPTER TWO

# MANX HISTORY

Since it's rare to see a tailless cat, you might be wondering about these kitties' history. How did they get their start? And where did they come from?

# A History Mystery

The Manx got its start on the Isle of Man. That's an island off England's west coast. No one is sure how the Manx got there though. Some say the Vikings brought it there.

A Viking ship like this one could have brought Manx cats to the Isle of Man.

Yet years ago, trading ships from many places often stopped at the island. Any one of these ships could have brought the cat there. So the Manx could have come to the island from just about anywhere. We may never know for sure.

This 1950 poster shows the Isle of Man with a Manx cat in the foreground.

# The Missing Tail

There are lots of stories about how the Manx lost its tail. None are true, but they are all interesting. In one story, the Manx started out with a tail. But the kitty stopped to catch a mouse on its way to Noah's ark. That's a famous ship in the Bible.

Just as it rushed on board, someone slammed the door shut. The cat made it in, but its tail did not. From then on, Manx cats had no tails.

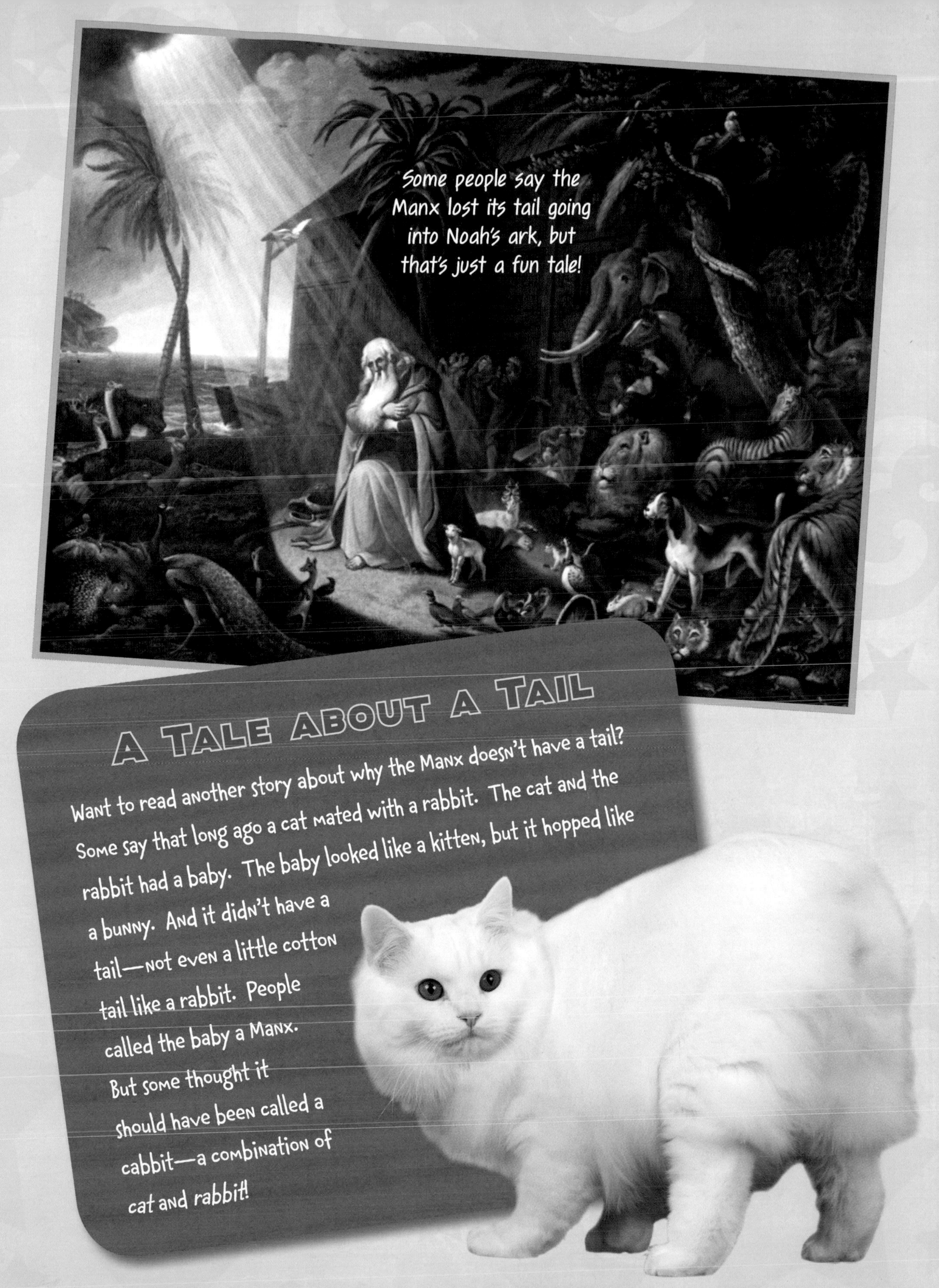


## A Tale about a Tail

Want to read another story about why the Manx doesn't have a tail? Some say that long ago a cat mated with a rabbit. The cat and the rabbit had a baby. The baby looked like a kitten, but it hopped like a bunny. And it didn't have a tail—not even a little cotton tail like a rabbit. People called the baby a Manx. But some thought it should have been called a cabbit—a combination of cat and rabbit!

# Then and Now

Early on, Manx cats caught the eye of royalty. In 1902, King Edward VII of Great Britain fell in love with the breed and adopted two Manx cats. They lived in his palaces and were treated very well.

King Edward VII enjoyed his Manx cats.

This Manx won a ribbon at a 2006 cat show in New York City.

The Manx was a hit in the United States too. During the 1930s, it won quite a few ribbons at cat shows. People found that Manx cats made great pets also. Before long, many American families had these pretty kitties in their homes.

## A Star from the Start

The first formal cat show was held in the Crystal Palace in London, England, on July 13, 1871. Thousands of people came and saw beautiful cats from all around the world. Among these was a lovely tailless cat that many people admired. You guessed it! It was the Manx.

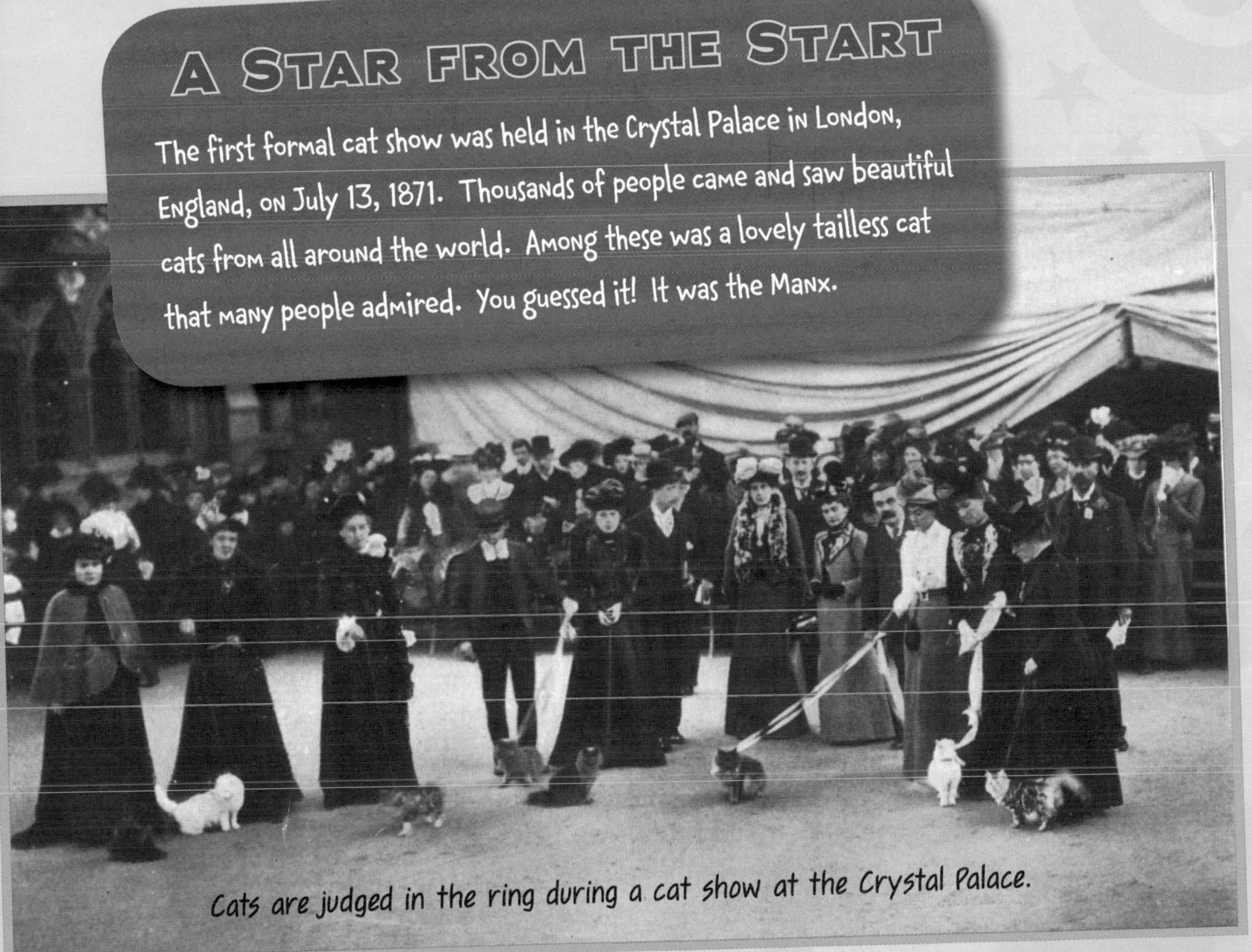

Cats are judged in the ring during a cat show at the Crystal Palace.

# CHAPTER THREE
# YOUR KIND OF CAT?

Manx cats are both intelligent and sweet. So should everybody get a Manx? The answer is no. No one pet is right for everyone. Read on to see if a Manx is right for you.

## Pride in Your Pet

You've got to be proud of your pet. The Manx is a wonderful cat—but be warned ahead of time. If you get one, you may get teased. Kids may say, "Isn't your cat missing something?" Or "Where did your cat leave its tail?" Not everyone thinks tailless cats are cute. How do you feel about it? Be sure of your feelings before getting a Manx.

# Action Cats

Are you looking for a quiet, laid-back cat? Do you long for a pet that looks good but doesn't need a lot of attention? If so, don't get a Manx.

Manx cats have a lot of energy!

Manx cats are active. They really love being with their owners. Many of these felines like to play ball. They can even be taught to fetch. Some can be leash-trained. And many enjoy car rides. If you don't like dogs, you might not like having a Manx.

This owner walks his Manx on a leash.

# A Costly Kitty

The Manx is a purebred cat. Manx kittens can be quite costly. Breeders may charge hundreds of dollars for one.

Can you afford a very high-priced pet? Discuss this with your family. Cost counts when it comes to adopting an animal.

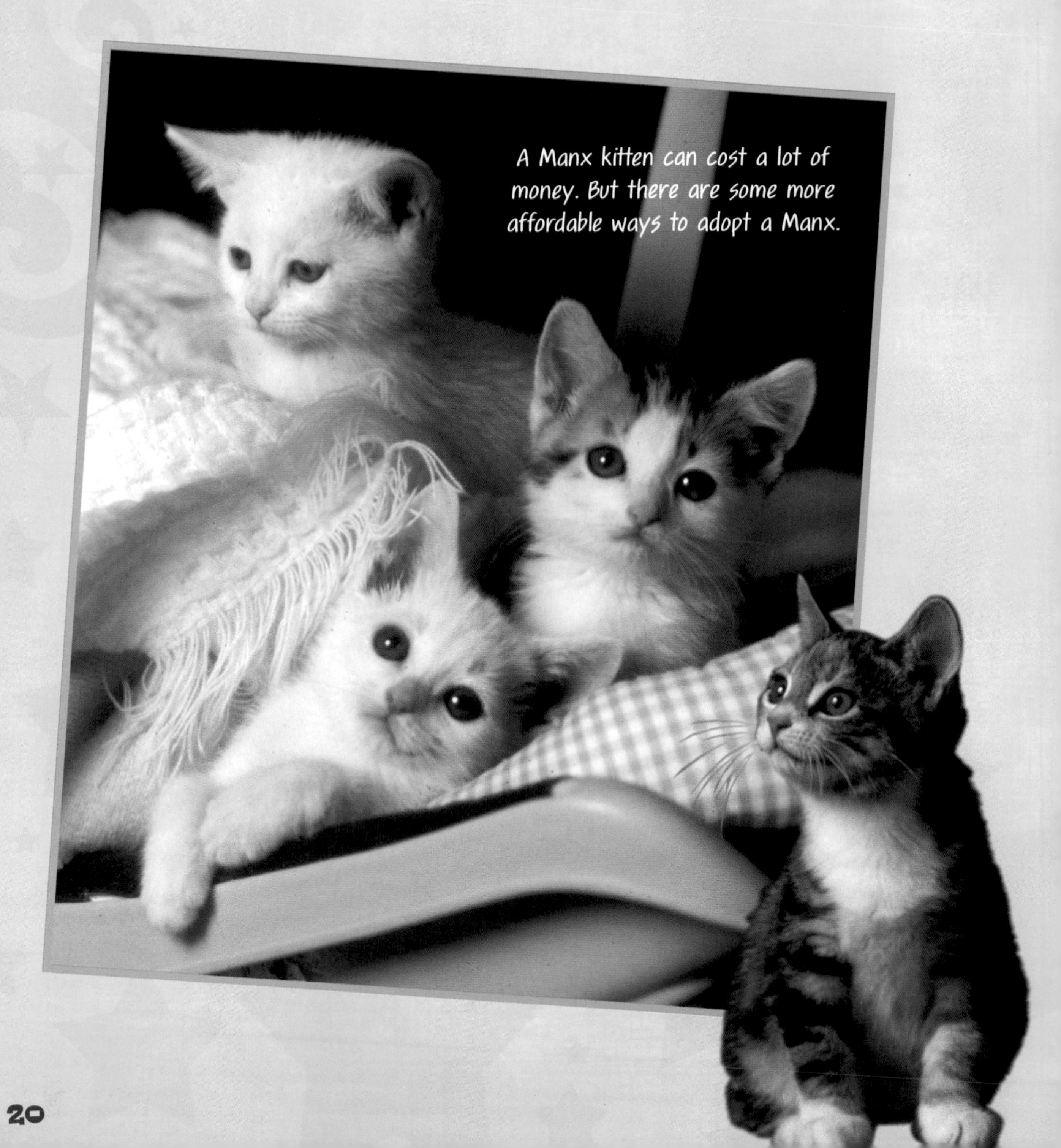

A Manx kitten can cost a lot of money. But there are some more affordable ways to adopt a Manx.

# Rescue a Manx

Can't afford a costly kitten? How about getting an older Manx? You can find these cats at rescue centers for this breed. Often you can get a lovely older cat for a low fee.

Just remember: All cats are costly. Even if you don't pay much for your pet, your family will still need to spend money on food and health care. But adopting a rescue cat can help you cut down on the purchase price.

You may find an older Manx at a rescue center.

Have you decided if a Manx is right for you? If it is, you've made a super choice. It would be hard to find a better kitty. People say that Manx cats are almost human. It's easy to fall for these fabulous felines.

## Is There a Mouse in the House?

If so, you've picked the right cat. Manx cats are great hunters and among the most marvelous mousers around. Many farmers use these cats to keep down the number of rodents.

CHAPTER FOUR

# HOME AT LAST

This day is going to be great. It isn't the last day of school. You're not going on vacation either. Something even better is happening. You're bringing your Manx home!

## Be Prepared

You have your camera ready. But you'll need more than that. Get these basic supplies before you get your cat.

- food and water bowls
- cat food
- litter box
- kitty litter
- brush and wide-tooth steel comb
- scratching post
- cat carrier

This Manx sits on top of a scratching post.

## Get to a Vet

Don't wait too long to take your cat to a veterinarian. That's a doctor who treats animals. They are called vets for short.

The vet will check your cat's health. Your kitty will also get the shots it needs. Be sure to take your cat back to the vet for regular checkups. Also take your Manx to the vet if it gets sick.

Veterinarians take care of many breeds of cats.

# Feeding Time

Ask your vet what to feed your cat. Be sure to stick to this diet. Don't share your ice cream or other snacks with your feline friend. This can lead to an unhealthful weight gain.

Be sure to feed your cat healthful food, and give it plenty of water to drink.

## Use Treats as Rewards

Don't give your Manx treats as snacks. Only use treats to reward good behavior. Did your cat just use the scratching post instead of tearing up the rug? Give that cat a treat!

# Grooming Your Cat

Brush and comb your Manx daily. This will remove any loose or dead hair from its coat. It will also help prevent matting.

## Manx Play

Manx cats love to play. You can find safe cat toys at most pet shops. Try a few, and see which your frisky kitty likes best.

Don't forget to brush your Manx to keep its fur looking great!

## You and Your Manx

You'll have tons of fun with your terrific cat. But be sure to take good care of your Manx too. Give it fresh food and water daily, and don't forget to groom it. You just may have the best cat ever. Be the best owner ever!

# GLOSSARY

**breed:** a particular type of cat. Cats of the same breed have the same body shape and general features.

**breeder:** someone who mates cats to produce a particular type of cat

**coat:** a cat's fur

**diet:** the food your cat eats

**feline:** a cat, or having to do with cats

**groom:** to clean, brush, and trim a cat's coat.

**matting:** severe tangling. Matting causes fur to clump together in large masses.

**purebred:** a cat whose parents are of the same breed

**rescue center:** a shelter where stray or abandoned cats are kept until they are adopted

**veterinarian:** a doctor who treats animals. Veterinarians are called vets for short.

# FOR MORE INFORMATION

## Books

Brecke, Nicole, and Patricia M. Stockland. *Cats You Can Draw.* Minneapolis: Millbrook Press, 2010. Perfect for cat lovers, this colorful book teaches readers how to draw many popular cat breeds.

Britton, Tamara L. *Manx Cats.* Edina, MN: Abdo, 2011. This easy-to-read book provides information on buying and living with a Manx.

Brown, Ruth. *Gracie the Lighthouse Cat.* London: Andersen Press, 2011. Gracie the lighthouse cat and Grace Darling, the lighthouse keeper's daughter, both have an adventure one very windy night.

Harris, Trudy. *Tally Cat Keeps Track.* Minneapolis: Millbrook Press, 2011. Tally McNally is a cat who loves to tally—but one day, he gets into a jam. Will his friends find a way to help him?

Landau, Elaine. *Your Pet Cat.* Rev. ed. New York: Children's Press, 2007. This title is a good guide for young people on choosing and caring for a cat.

## Websites

### ASPCA Kids

**http://www.aspca.org/aspcakids**

Check out this website for helpful hints on caring for a cat and other pets.

### For Kids: About Cats

**http://kids.cfa.org**

Be sure to visit this fun website for kids on cats and cat shows. Don't miss the links to some fun games as well.

# Index



# Photo Acknowledgments

The images in this book are used with the permission of: © iStockphoto.com/Michael Balderas, p. 1; © iStockphoto.com/Julie Fisher and © iStockphoto.com/javarman3 (all backgrounds); © Photos by Chanan, pp. 4, 5 (both), 6, 6-7, 7, 9 (both), 10 (bottom), 12, 13 (bottom), 14 (top), 20; © Fiona Green, pp. 8, 16, 17, 18, 19, 24 (left), 25, 27 (both), 28, 29; © North Wind Picture Archives, p. 10 (top); © Science & Society/SuperStock, pp. 10-11; The Granger Collection, New York, p. 13 (top); The Art Archive/Private Collection MD, p. 14 (bottom); AP Photo/Shiho Fukada, p. 15 (top); The Department of Rare Books and Special Collections, University of Michigan Library, p. 15 (bottom); © J-L. & M-L. Hubert/Photolibrary, pp. 18-19; © Yann Arthus-Bertrand/CORBIS, pp. 20-21; © Jesse A. Wanskasmith/First Light/Glow Images, p. 21; © Mark J. Barrett/Alamy, p. 22; © Ron Kimball/www.kimballstock.com, p. 23; © Agita Leimane/Dreamstime.com, p. 24 (top right); © Mark Bond/Dreamstime.com, p. 24 (middle right); © Eti Swinford/Dreamstime.com, p. 24 (bottom right); © Stoyan Nenov/Reuters/CORBIS, p. 26 (top); © Ariel Skelley/Blend Images/Getty Images, p. 26 (bottom).

Front Cover: © J-L. Klein & M-L. Hubert/Bios/Photolibrary.
Back Cover: © Juniors Bildarchiv/Alamy.